LISTEN, My Children, and You Shall Hear

(BOOK 1 — REVISED)

*A manual of stories and exercises
designed to help children develop listening
skills, auditory memory, vocabulary and imagination*

Pre-school Through Grade Four

LISTEN, My Children, and You Shall Hear

(BOOK 1 — REVISED)

Betty Lou Kratoville

The Interstate Printers & Publishers, Inc.

DANVILLE, ILLINOIS

Library of Congress Catalog Card No. 87-80891

ISBN 0-8134-2757-6

1 2 3
4 5 6
7 8 9

Who else but for Matthew!

INTRODUCTION

The ability of a child to perceive the world by sight, sound and touch is receiving widespread attention by educators. It is now generally accepted that faulty perception is one of the basic causative factors of learning disabilities. This has resulted in specialization in the field by ever-increasing numbers of professionals—e.g., developmental optometrists, audiologists and speech-language pathologists. Standardized tests have been developed, and many children whose problems have heretofore gone undiagnosed are now identified as having perceptual disabilities.

Diagnosis is one thing; remediation is quite another. In the field of visual perception, much has been done to provide the teacher or the parent with specific programs and tools of remediation. One need only consult the literature in the field to find an abundance of excellent materials for classroom or home. Thus far in the area of auditory perceptual problems, a paucity of materials exists, and this manual has been designed to aid in filling that gap and to provide a program of remediation for pre-school children and for those in the primary grades.

TABLE OF CONTENTS

SECTION ONE:

Instructions for Use of the Stories

Stories

INSTRUCTIONS FOR USE OF THE STORIES

Technique

Each of the following stories should be read aloud to the child at a moderate speed with little emphasis. The child should then be instructed to "tell the story."

Selecting the proper level for the individual child is highly important. The material should be challenging but not so difficult that the child is immediately discouraged. It is suggested that the instructor begin at the "First Level." If the child can perform there with no difficulty, the "Second Level" should be used. If this is too simple, the instructor should move on to the "Third Level." Once the proper level is established, that same level should be used for each story until the child is ready to move to a higher level.

No more than three stories should be read and re-told in one auditory memory training period. It is further suggested that at least a two-month interval elapse before a story is repeated. In this way it is unlikely that the child will *memorize* a story. It is important to keep in mind that these stories are designed to develop *immediate* auditory recall and should not be used for long-range memory work.

All terms should be familiar to the child. For example, in the story which refers to a broken arm and a cast, the word "cast" should be explained and discussed if the child has had no experience with broken bones. For the most part, the stories refer to common events, places and things, but occasionally an uncommon element has been included in an effort to widen the child's horizon.

These stories should also be used to develop verbalization and imagination. After the child has repeated a story, the instructor may ask: "What do you suppose happened then?" or, "What would you do if this were you?" or, "Has anything like this ever happened to you?"

It has been found that a child may want to "turn the tables" on the instructor, to tell a story of his or her own and to ask the instructor to repeat it. This should be encouraged but only after the child has completed the regular assignment.

Occasionally, if the story seems to pertain to the child, his or her name may be inserted in the text. Children like to hear or tell stories about themselves, and this can be an excellent device to gain their attention and interest.

As part of the activity, the child may be asked to draw a single picture or a series of pictures, comic-strip style, illustrating the story, or one or more children may be invited to "act out" the sequence of events.

Grading

Space has been provided to grade the child on each performance. A rating of "Good" would indicate that the child has been able to repeat 75 percent or more of the story; "Fair" would indicate between 50 and 75 percent; "Poor" would indicate 50 percent or less and would suggest that perhaps a lower level should be used. The child should *not* know he or she is being graded. Grading is merely to provide the instructor with a basis for comparison from one month to the next. The date should also be noted next to the grade.

In a classroom situation, the teacher may wish to keep accurate individual records in a separate notebook by assigning a page to each child. Specially designed grading sheets for this purpose are available in packs of 20 from The Interstate Printers & Publishers, Inc., Danville, Illinois (reorder no. 1045).

1

FIRST LEVEL

A little boy went for a walk. He saw a mud puddle. He jumped into it. Then he went home and
took a bath.

Good_____
Fair_____
Poor_____

SECOND LEVEL

A little boy went for a walk. He saw a mud puddle. He jumped into it. Up and down, up and
down, up and down he jumped, three times.
Then he went home and took a bath.

Good_____
Fair_____
Poor_____

THIRD LEVEL

After the rain stopped, a little boy went for a
walk. He saw a brown mud puddle. He jumped
into it. Up and down, up and down, up and down
he jumped, three times. Then he went home and
took a warm bath.

Good_____
Fair_____
Poor_____

2

FIRST LEVEL

A boy and his mother took a ride in a car. They saw a long train. A man in the red caboose waved at them.

Good_____
Fair_____
Poor_____

SECOND LEVEL

A boy and his mother took a ride in a car. They saw a long train. There was a man in the red caboose. He waved at the little boy.

Good_____
Fair_____
Poor_____

THIRD LEVEL

A boy and his mother took a ride in a car. They stopped at a railroad crossing to watch a long train pass by. There was a man in the red caboose. He waved at the little boy. The boy waved back.

Good_____
Fair_____
Poor_____

3

FIRST LEVEL

A little girl woke up one morning. She looked out
of her bedroom window. Big white snowflakes
were falling.

Good_____
Fair_____
Poor_____

SECOND LEVEL

A little girl woke up one morning. She looked out
of her bedroom window. Big white snowflakes
were falling. She put on her coat and boots and
mittens and went outside.

Good_____
Fair_____
Poor_____

THIRD LEVEL

A little girl woke up one morning. She looked out
of her bedroom window. Big white snowflakes
were falling. After breakfast, she put on her coat
and boots and mittens and went outside. She
made two snowpeople.

Good_____
Fair_____
Poor_____

4

FIRST LEVEL

Two monkeys lived in a zoo. They liked to swing by their tails and scratch their heads and eat peanuts.

Good_____
Fair_____
Poor_____

SECOND LEVEL

Two monkeys lived in a zoo. They liked to swing by their tails and scratch their heads. They liked the children who gave them peanuts to eat.

Good_____
Fair_____
Poor_____

THIRD LEVEL

Two monkeys lived in a zoo. They liked to swing by their tails and scratch their heads. They liked Sunday afternoons when many children visited the zoo and gave them peanuts to eat.

Good_____
Fair_____
Poor_____

5

FIRST LEVEL

A mother asked her little boy if he wanted to go
to the grocery store with her. The little boy said,
"Oh, yes."

Good_____
Fair_____
Poor_____

SECOND LEVEL

A mother asked her little boy if he wanted to go
to the store with her. The little boy said, "Oh,
yes." They went to the grocery store and bought
milk and bread.

Good_____
Fair_____
Poor_____

THIRD LEVEL

A mother asked her little boy if he wanted to go
to the store with her. The little boy said, "Oh,
yes." First they went to the grocery store and
bought milk and bread. Then they went to the
drugstore and drank chocolate sodas.

Good_____
Fair_____
Poor_____

6

FIRST LEVEL

A little girl was running. She fell down and hurt
her knee. Her mother put a bandage on it.

Good_____
Fair_____
Poor_____

SECOND LEVEL

A little girl was running. She fell down and hurt
her knee. Her mother washed it and put a bandage on it. It felt much better.

Good_____
Fair_____
Poor_____

THIRD LEVEL

A little girl was running on the sidewalk. She fell
down and hurt her knee. Her mother washed it
and put a bandage on it. It felt much better, so
the little girl went back outside to play.

Good_____
Fair_____
Poor_____

7

FIRST LEVEL

Three brothers got on a yellow school bus. It took
them to school in the morning and brought them
home in the afternoon.

Good_____
Fair_____
Poor_____

SECOND LEVEL

Three brothers got on a yellow school bus. It took
them to school in the morning and brought them
home in the afternoon. The bus driver was a
friendly person.

Good_____
Fair_____
Poor_____

THIRD LEVEL

Three brothers got on a yellow school bus. It took
them to school. One brother was in kindergarten,
one was in first grade and one was in fourth
grade. In the afternoon the bus brought them
back home. The driver was a friendly person.

Good_____
Fair_____
Poor_____

8

FIRST LEVEL

Two white rabbits ran through the woods. They saw a hole and climbed into it to take a nap.

Good_____
Fair_____
Poor_____

SECOND LEVEL

Two white rabbits ran through the woods. They saw a hole and climbed into it to take a nap. Later they found two carrots and ate them up.

Good_____
Fair_____
Poor_____

THIRD LEVEL

Two white rabbits ran through the woods. They saw a hole and climbed into it to rest. One rabbit said, "It is dark in here." The other rabbit said, "Let's climb out and look for a carrot." They found two carrots and ate them up.

Good_____
Fair_____
Poor_____

9

FIRST LEVEL

Two frogs lived under a stone. In the winter they slept and kept warm. In the summer they played with their frog friends.

Good_____
Fair_____
Poor_____

SECOND LEVEL

Two frogs lived under a stone by the side of the road. In the winter they slept and kept warm. In the summer they played leapfrog with their friends.

Good_____
Fair_____
Poor_____

THIRD LEVEL

Two frogs lived under a stone by the side of the road. In the winter they slept and kept warm. In the summer they played leapfrog with their friends and caught flies for their supper.

Good_____
Fair_____
Poor_____

10

FIRST LEVEL

A sleepy puppy lay down on the floor to take a nap. A kitty crept up softly and tickled the puppy's chin.

Good_____
Fair_____
Poor_____

SECOND LEVEL

The puppy was sleepy. It lay down on the floor to take a nap. A kitty crept up softly and tickled the puppy's chin. The puppy woke up.

Good_____
Fair_____
Poor_____

THIRD LEVEL

The puppy was sleepy. It lay down on the floor to take a nap. A kitty crept up softly and tickled the puppy's chin. The puppy woke up and chased the kitty but could not catch it.

Good_____
Fair_____
Poor_____

11

FIRST LEVEL

A family went to the beach. Everyone helped to make a picnic lunch. The father and the mother went fishing with the children.

Good_____
Fair_____
Poor_____

SECOND LEVEL

A family went to the beach. Everyone helped to make a picnic lunch. The father and the mother went fishing with the children. Then the whole family built castles in the sand and splashed in the waves.

Good_____
Fair_____
Poor_____

THIRD LEVEL

A family went to the beach. Everyone helped to make a picnic lunch. The father and the mother went fishing with the children. Then the whole family built castles in the sand and splashed in the waves. When they were all tired, they went home.

Good_____
Fair_____
Poor_____

12

FIRST LEVEL

A little boy with muddy shoes came into the house. His mother said, "Oh, dear. I just mopped the floor."

Good_____
Fair_____
Poor_____

SECOND LEVEL

A little boy with muddy shoes came into the house. His mother said, "Oh, dear. I just mopped the floor, and now it is all dirty again." The little boy was sorry.

Good_____
Fair_____
Poor_____

THIRD LEVEL

A little boy with muddy shoes came into the house. His mother said, "Oh, dear. I just mopped the floor, and now it is all dirty again." The little boy was sorry, so he got a mop. Soon the floor was bright and clean.

Good_____
Fair_____
Poor_____

13

FIRST LEVEL

A little girl woke up in the morning. She did not feel well. She stayed in bed. The next day she was better.

Good_____
Fair_____
Poor_____

SECOND LEVEL

A little girl woke up in the morning. She did not feel well and did not want her breakfast. She stayed in bed all day. The next day she was better.

Good_____
Fair_____
Poor_____

THIRD LEVEL

A little girl woke up in the morning. She did not feel well and did not want her breakfast. Her father took her temperature. The little girl stayed in bed all day and drank lots of ginger ale. The next day she was better.

Good_____
Fair_____
Poor_____

14

FIRST LEVEL

The family was fixing dinner. The little girl wanted strawberry jello for dessert. Her brother wanted bananas.

Good_____
Fair_____
Poor_____

SECOND LEVEL

The little girl wanted strawberry jello for dessert. Her brother wanted sliced bananas. Their mother said, "Let's make strawberry jello with sliced bananas in it."

Good_____
Fair_____
Poor_____

THIRD LEVEL

The little girl wanted strawberry jello for dessert. Her brother wanted sliced bananas. Their mother said, "Let's make strawberry jello with sliced bananas in it, and then you both will be happy." The girl and the boy said, "Thank you, Mother."

Good_____
Fair_____
Poor_____

15

FIRST LEVEL

On the Fourth of July the children decorated their bicycles with red, white and blue paper. They rode the bicycles in a parade.

Good_____
Fair_____
Poor_____

SECOND LEVEL

On the Fourth of July the children decorated their bicycles with red, white and blue paper. They rode the bicycles in a parade. When it was dark, they watched the bright fireworks.

Good_____
Fair_____
Poor_____

THIRD LEVEL

On the Fourth of July the children decorated their bicycles with red, white and blue paper. They rode the bicycles in a parade. Later good friends came for a picnic supper. When it was dark, everyone watched the bright, beautiful fireworks.

Good_____
Fair_____
Poor_____

16

FIRST LEVEL

The little boy wanted to be helpful. His mother
asked him to pick up his toys, and he did. He
helped his sister wash the car.

Good_____
Fair_____
Poor_____

SECOND LEVEL

The little boy wanted to be helpful. His mother
asked him to pick up his toys, and he did. His sister asked him to help wash the car, and he did.
Then he ate a cookie.

Good_____
Fair_____
Poor_____

THIRD LEVEL

The little boy wanted to be helpful. His mother
said, "You may pick up your toys." And he did.
His sister said, "You may help me wash the car."
And he did. His grandmother said, "You may
help me eat some cookies." And he did.

Good_____
Fair_____
Poor_____

17

FIRST LEVEL

The little girl wanted some chocolate milk. Her mother poured chocolate syrup into a glass of milk and stirred it. The little girl drank every drop.

Good_____
Fair_____
Poor_____

SECOND LEVEL

The little girl wanted some chocolate milk. Her mother poured chocolate syrup into a glass of milk and stirred it with a spoon. It tasted very good, and the little girl drank every drop.

Good_____
Fair_____
Poor_____

THIRD LEVEL

The little girl wanted some chocolate milk. Her mother poured chocolate syrup into a glass of white milk and stirred it with a spoon. It tasted very good, and the little girl quickly drank it all up. Then she washed and dried her glass and put it in the cupboard.

Good_____
Fair_____
Poor_____

18

FIRST LEVEL

The boy's shoes were too small. His father took him to the shoe store. The boy picked out brown shoes for school.

Good_____
Fair_____
Poor_____

SECOND LEVEL

The boy's shoes were too small. His father took him to the shoe store. The boy picked out brown shoes for school and black shoes for special occasions.

Good_____
Fair_____
Poor_____

THIRD LEVEL

The boy's shoes were too small. His father took him to the shoe store. The boy picked out brown shoes for school, black shoes for special occasions and white sneakers for play. He wore the sneakers home.

Good_____
Fair_____
Poor_____

19

FIRST LEVEL

The boy wanted to know all about kittens. His father said, "Kittens are very tiny, so we must be gentle with them."

Good_____
Fair_____
Poor_____

SECOND LEVEL

The boy wanted to know all about kittens. His father said, "Kittens are very tiny, so we must be gentle with them. Kittens like to play with catnip toys and take long naps."

Good_____
Fair_____
Poor_____

THIRD LEVEL

The boy wanted to know all about kittens. His father said, "Kittens are very tiny and very delicate, so we must be gentle with them. Kittens like to play with catnip toys and take long naps. They like to sit in the laps of friendly children."

Good_____
Fair_____
Poor_____

20

FIRST LEVEL

One afternoon the little boy and his father went to a pet store. They saw three fat brown-and-white puppies.

Good_____
Fair_____
Poor_____

SECOND LEVEL

One afternoon the little boy and his father went to a pet store. They saw three fat puppies—a brown one, a black one and a white one. They took the brown puppy home with them.

Good_____
Fair_____
Poor_____

THIRD LEVEL

One afternoon the little boy and his father went to a pet store. They saw three fat puppies—a brown one, a black one and a white one. The little boy liked the brown puppy best because it licked his fingers. He and his father took the brown puppy home with them.

Good_____
Fair_____
Poor_____

21

FIRST LEVEL

The ice-cream man drove down the street in his little white truck. The children all bought popsicles.

Good____
Fair____
Poor____

SECOND LEVEL

The ice-cream man drove down the street in his little white truck. The children ran into their houses and asked their parents for money. Then they all bought popsicles.

Good____
Fair____
Poor____

THIRD LEVEL

The ice-cream man drove down the street in his little white truck. The children ran into their houses and asked their parents for money. Then they all bought popsicles. The truck clanged its bell and drove away.

Good____
Fair____
Poor____

22

FIRST LEVEL

The teacher asked the children which holiday they liked best. A little girl said, "I like Christmas and presents."

Good_____
Fair_____
Poor_____

SECOND LEVEL

The teacher asked the children which holiday they liked best. A little boy said, "I like Halloween and tricks or treats." A little girl said, "I like Christmas and presents."

Good_____
Fair_____
Poor_____

THIRD LEVEL

The teacher asked the children which holiday they liked best. A little boy said, "I like Halloween and tricks or treats." Another boy said, "I like Thanksgiving and turkey." A little girl said, "I like Christmas and presents."

Good_____
Fair_____
Poor_____

23

FIRST LEVEL

The little boy was invited to stay all night with his best friend. He packed his pajamas and his toothbrush in a suitcase.

Good_____
Fair_____
Poor_____

SECOND LEVEL

The little boy was invited to stay all night with his best friend. He packed his pajamas and his toothbrush in a suitcase. Then he kissed his mother and father good-bye.

Good_____
Fair_____
Poor_____

THIRD LEVEL

The little boy was invited to stay all night with his best friend. He packed his pajamas and his robe and his toothbrush in a suitcase. Then he kissed his mother and father good-bye. The next morning, after breakfast, he came home.

Good_____
Fair_____
Poor_____

24

FIRST LEVEL

A little boy had a toothache. His mother took him to the dentist. The dentist fixed the tooth so it didn't hurt any more.

Good_____
Fair_____
Poor_____

SECOND LEVEL

A little boy had a toothache. His mother took him to the dentist. The dentist fixed the tooth so it didn't hurt any more and then cleaned the boy's teeth.

Good_____
Fair_____
Poor_____

THIRD LEVEL

A little boy had a toothache. His mother took him to the dentist. The dentist fixed the tooth so it didn't hurt any more and then cleaned the boy's teeth. The dentist said, "Remember to brush your teeth after every meal."

Good_____
Fair_____
Poor_____

25

FIRST LEVEL

A girl and a boy decided to build a doghouse.
When it was finished, they painted it red and
white.

Good_____
Fair_____
Poor_____

SECOND LEVEL

A girl and a boy decided to build a doghouse. The
girl got some wood and nails. The boy found a
hammer and a saw. Soon the doghouse was
finished.

Good_____
Fair_____
Poor_____

THIRD LEVEL

A girl and a boy decided to build a doghouse. The
girl got some wood and nails. The boy found a
hammer and a saw. They worked very hard.
When the doghouse was finished, they painted it
red and white.

Good_____
Fair_____
Poor_____

26

FIRST LEVEL

The little girl was invited to a birthday party. She
put on her pink dress and pink socks and shiny
black shoes.

Good_____
Fair_____
Poor_____

SECOND LEVEL

The little girl was invited to a birthday party. She
put on her pink dress and pink socks and shiny
black shoes. Her mother tied a pink ribbon in her
hair.

Good_____
Fair_____
Poor_____

THIRD LEVEL

The little girl was invited to a birthday party. She
put on her pink dress and pink socks and shiny
black shoes. Her mother tied a pink ribbon in her
hair. The little girl wrapped a present in pretty
paper to take to the party.

Good_____
Fair_____
Poor_____

27

FIRST LEVEL

The boy had a loose tooth. His mother wiggled it
gently, and it popped out. That night the good
fairy came and left 10 pennies.

Good_____
Fair_____
Poor_____

SECOND LEVEL

The boy had a loose tooth. His mother wiggled it
gently, and it popped out. He put it under his pil-
low. That night the good fairy came and took the
tooth and left 10 pennies.

Good_____
Fair_____
Poor_____

THIRD LEVEL

The boy had a loose tooth. His mother wiggled it
gently, and it popped out. He put it under his pil-
low. That night, while he was sleeping, the good
fairy came and took the tooth and left one dime,
one nickel and five pennies.

Good_____
Fair_____
Poor_____

28

FIRST LEVEL

A fat frog jumped into a swimming pool. It could
not get out. A friendly boy caught it in a net and
let it jump away.

Good_____
Fair_____
Poor_____

SECOND LEVEL

A fat frog jumped into a swimming pool. It could
not get out. A friendly boy caught it in a net and
let it jump away to its home in the nearby woods.

Good_____
Fair_____
Poor_____

THIRD LEVEL

A fat frog jumped into a swimming pool by mis-
take. It tried very hard to get out, but it could
not. It was happy when a friendly boy caught it in
a net and let it jump away to its home in the nearby woods.

Good_____
Fair_____
Poor_____

29

FIRST LEVEL

A mother asked three boys what they wanted for
breakfast. They all wanted cereal and pancakes
and eggs.

Good_____
Fair_____
Poor_____

SECOND LEVEL

A mother asked three boys what they wanted for
breakfast. One boy wanted cereal. One boy wanted pancakes. One boy wanted eggs.

Good_____
Fair_____
Poor_____

THIRD LEVEL

A mother asked three boys what they wanted for
breakfast. The first boy said, "I want cereal." The
second boy said, "I want cereal and pancakes."
The third boy said, "I want cereal and pancakes
and eggs."

Good_____
Fair_____
Poor_____

30

FIRST LEVEL

The boy and his father went to a big department
store. They rode up to the second floor on an ele-
vator. Then they walked around and looked at
toys.

Good_____
Fair_____
Poor_____

SECOND LEVEL

The boy and his father went to a big department
store. They rode up to the second floor on an ele-
vator. They walked around and looked at toys.
Then they rode down to the first floor on an esca-
lator.

Good_____
Fair_____
Poor_____

THIRD LEVEL

The boy and his father went to a big department
store. They rode up to the second floor on an ele-
vator. They walked around and looked at toys.
Then they rode down to the first floor on an esca-
lator. The boy said, "This is more fun than walk-
ing down stairs."

Good_____
Fair_____
Poor_____

31

FIRST LEVEL

On Sunday afternoon a little boy and his sister
took a walk in the woods. They saw a squirrel
climb a tall tree.

Good____
Fair____
Poor____

SECOND LEVEL

On Sunday afternoon a little boy and his sister
took a walk in the woods. They saw a brown
squirrel climb a tall tree. They saw a white rabbit
run into the bushes.

Good____
Fair____
Poor____

THIRD LEVEL

On Sunday afternoon a little boy and his sister
took a walk in the woods. They saw a brown
squirrel climb a tall tree. They saw a white rabbit
run into the bushes. They saw a wiggly snake
crawl across the path.

Good____
Fair____
Poor____

32

FIRST LEVEL

A little girl wanted to pick blackberries. She
walked to the blackberry patch and filled a pan
with berries. She ate them for dessert.

Good_____
Fair_____
Poor_____

SECOND LEVEL

A little girl wanted to pick blackberries. Her father gave her a pan. She walked to the blackberry
patch and filled the pan with berries. She and her
family ate them for dessert.

Good_____
Fair_____
Poor_____

THIRD LEVEL

A little girl wanted to pick blackberries. Her father gave her a pan. She walked to the blackberry
patch and filled the pan with berries. Her father
washed them and put sugar on them. The girl and
her family ate them for dessert.

Good_____
Fair_____
Poor_____

33

FIRST LEVEL

The boy had a rip in his pajamas. His mother
mended the rip with a needle and white thread.
The pajamas were good as new.

Good_____
Fair_____
Poor_____

SECOND LEVEL

The boy had a rip in his pajamas. His mother put
on her thimble and used a needle and white
thread to mend the rip. When she was finished,
the pajamas were good as new.

Good_____
Fair_____
Poor_____

THIRD LEVEL

The boy had a rip in his pajamas. His mother took
a red thimble and a needle and white thread from
her sewing basket. She carefully mended the rip.
When she was finished, the pajamas were good as
new. The boy wore them to bed that night.

Good_____
Fair_____
Poor_____

34

FIRST LEVEL

The father and the boy talked about good manners. The boy learned to say "thank you" and "you're welcome."

Good_____
Fair_____
Poor_____

SECOND LEVEL

The father said, "Let's talk about good manners. You should learn to say 'thank you' and 'you're welcome.'" The boy said he would try to remember.

Good_____
Fair_____
Poor_____

THIRD LEVEL

The father said, "Let's talk about good manners. You should learn to say 'please,' 'thank you' and 'you're welcome.'" The boy said, "Thank you for teaching me. I'll try to remember."

Good_____
Fair_____
Poor_____

35

FIRST LEVEL

Three little pigs lived on a farm. They liked to eat
vegetables and nuts and to play in the soft mud.

Good____
Fair____
Poor____

SECOND LEVEL

Three little pigs lived on a farm. They liked to eat
vegetables and nuts and to play in the soft mud.
They squealed, "Oink, oink, oink!" when the farm
dog chased them.

Good____
Fair____
Poor____

THIRD LEVEL

Three little pigs lived on a farm. They liked to eat
vegetables and nuts and to play in the soft mud.
Sometimes the farm dog chased them. Then they
ran to their mother and father and squealed,
"Oink, oink, oink!"

Good____
Fair____
Poor____

36

FIRST LEVEL

In winter it is very cold. In spring it is warm. In summer it is very hot. In autumn it is cool.

Good_____
Fair_____
Poor_____

SECOND LEVEL

Each year has four seasons. Cold winter comes first. Next comes warm spring. Then hot summer comes. Last to come is autumn, which is cool.

Good_____
Fair_____
Poor_____

THIRD LEVEL

Each year has four seasons. Cold winter comes first. Next comes spring, which is warm. Then comes summer, which is hot. Last to come is autumn, which is cool. Then the year starts all over again.

Good_____
Fair_____
Poor_____

37

FIRST LEVEL

A clock tells us when it is time to go to school and
when it is time to come home. A clock has 12
numbers on its face.

Good____
Fair____
Poor____

SECOND LEVEL

A clock tells us when it is time to go to school and
when it is time to come home. It tells us when it
is time for supper and when it is time to go to
bed. A clock has 12 numbers on its face.

Good____
Fair____
Poor____

THIRD LEVEL

A clock tells us when it is time to go to school and
when it is time to come home. It tells us when it
is time for supper and when it is time to go to
bed. A clock has 12 numbers on its face. There
are many different kinds of clocks.

Good____
Fair____
Poor____

38

FIRST LEVEL

The boy and his father went shopping for school clothes. They bought jeans and shirts and a sweater.

Good____
Fair____
Poor____

SECOND LEVEL

At the end of summer, Father said, "Soon it will be time for school to start." He took his little boy shopping for school clothes. They bought jeans and shirts and a sweater.

Good____
Fair____
Poor____

THIRD LEVEL

At the end of summer, Father said, "Soon it will be time for school to start." He took his little boy to a department store to shop for school clothes. They bought three pair of jeans, four shirts, one sweater and a yellow raincoat.

Good____
Fair____
Poor____

39

FIRST LEVEL

The carrier delivered the mail. There was a letter for Father and a magazine for Mother and a package for the little girl.

Good_____
Fair_____
Poor_____

SECOND LEVEL

The carrier delivered the mail. There was a letter for Father and a magazine for Mother and a package for the little girl. The girl unwrapped the package. Inside was a new book.

Good_____
Fair_____
Poor_____

THIRD LEVEL

The carrier delivered the mail. There was a letter for Father and a magazine for Mother. Also, there was a package for the little girl from her grandmother. She unwrapped the package. Inside was a new book of stories and poems.

Good_____
Fair_____
Poor_____

40

FIRST LEVEL

The father asked the little boy about his day in school. The little boy said, "We sang some songs and had milk and cookies."

Good_____
Fair_____
Poor_____

SECOND LEVEL

The father asked the little boy about his day in kindergarten. The little boy said, "We sang some songs and had milk and cookies. Next we drew a picture of a house with our crayons."

Good_____
Fair_____
Poor_____

THIRD LEVEL

The father asked the little boy about his day in kindergarten. The little boy said, "We sang some songs and had milk and cookies. Next we drew a picture of a house with our crayons. Then we went outside to the playground to play games."

Good_____
Fair_____
Poor_____

41

FIRST LEVEL

Three brown squirrels lived in a tree. They had
long, bushy tails. They gathered nuts to eat in the
wintertime.

Good_____
Fair_____
Poor_____

SECOND LEVEL

Three brown squirrels lived in a tree. They had
long, bushy tails and sharp little teeth. They
gathered nuts to eat in the wintertime. They liked
to chase one another over the rooftops.

Good_____
Fair_____
Poor_____

THIRD LEVEL

Three brown squirrels lived in a tall oak tree.
They had long, bushy tails and sharp little teeth.
They gathered acorns and pecans to eat in the
wintertime. They liked to chase one another
through the trees and over the rooftops.

Good_____
Fair_____
Poor_____

42

FIRST LEVEL

Some workers were building a house. When it was all finished, a family with four children moved into the new house.

Good_____
Fair_____
Poor_____

SECOND LEVEL

Some workers were building a house. First they dug a hole and poured in cement. Then they nailed up a frame of wood and covered it with bricks. Later a family with four children moved into the new house.

Good_____
Fair_____
Poor_____

THIRD LEVEL

Some workers were building a house. First they dug a large hole and poured in cement. Then they nailed up a frame of wood and covered it with bricks. They put in doors and windows. When the new house was finished, a family with four children moved into it.

Good_____
Fair_____
Poor_____

43

FIRST LEVEL

The mother baked a chocolate cake and put pink icing on it. She let her little boy lick the bowl and spoon.

Good_____
Fair_____
Poor_____

SECOND LEVEL

The mother baked a chocolate cake and put pink icing on it. She let her little boy lick the icing bowl and spoon. When he was finished, he washed his sticky fingers.

Good_____
Fair_____
Poor_____

THIRD LEVEL

The mother baked a two-layer chocolate cake and put pink icing on it. She let her little boy lick the icing bowl and spoon. When he was finished, he washed his sticky fingers. That night the family ate the cake at supper.

Good_____
Fair_____
Poor_____

44

FIRST LEVEL

All children should know three important things—name, address and telephone number.

Good_____
Fair_____
Poor_____

SECOND LEVEL

All children should know three important things—name, address and telephone number. Then, if they should get lost, a friendly police officer can call their parents or take them home.

Good_____
Fair_____
Poor_____

THIRD LEVEL

All children should know three important things—name, address and telephone number. Then, if they should get lost, they can tell a friendly police officer who they are, where they live and what their telephone number is. The police officer can call their parents or take them home.

Good_____
Fair_____
Poor_____

45

FIRST LEVEL

The mother wrote a letter to the grandmother.
She put it in an envelope and put a stamp on it.

Good_____
Fair_____
Poor_____

SECOND LEVEL

The mother wrote a letter to the grandmother.
She put it in an envelope and put a stamp on it.
Then she asked her little girl to drop it in the
mailbox on the corner.

Good_____
Fair_____
Poor_____

THIRD LEVEL

The mother wrote a letter to the grandmother.
She put it in an envelope and put a stamp on it.
Then she gave it to her little girl to mail. The girl
walked to a mailbox on the corner and dropped
the letter into it.

Good_____
Fair_____
Poor_____

46

FIRST LEVEL

The boy and his father made a garden. They put
seeds in the soft dirt. In the summer red flowers
bloomed in the garden.

Good_____
Fair_____
Poor_____

SECOND LEVEL

The boy and his father made a garden. They put
seeds in the soft dirt. Soon little green plants ap-
peared. The boy watered them, and in the summer red flowers bloomed in the garden.

Good_____
Fair_____
Poor_____

THIRD LEVEL

The boy and his father made a garden. They put
seeds in the soft dirt. Soon little green plants ap-
peared. The boy watered and weeded the garden.
The plants grew taller, and one day red flowers
bloomed on them.

Good_____
Fair_____
Poor_____

47

FIRST LEVEL

The little boy was tired. He took a warm bath. Then he put on his pajamas and got into bed. He quickly fell asleep.

Good_____
Fair_____
Poor_____

SECOND LEVEL

The little boy was tired. He took a warm bath. Then he put on his pajamas and brushed his teeth. He kissed his mother and father goodnight. He quickly fell asleep.

Good_____
Fair_____
Poor_____

THIRD LEVEL

At seven o'clock the little boy was tired. He took a warm bath. Then he put on his pajamas and brushed his teeth. He kissed his mother and father goodnight and got into bed. He quickly fell asleep.

Good_____
Fair_____
Poor_____

48

FIRST LEVEL

A boy and his sister went for a walk to their cousin's house. On the way they saw two dogs and
three squirrels.

Good_____
Fair_____
Poor_____

SECOND LEVEL

A boy and his sister went for a walk to their cousin's house. On the way they saw two dogs and
three squirrels and one kitten. The squirrels ran
away, but the dogs and the kitten were friendly.

Good_____
Fair_____
Poor_____

THIRD LEVEL

One sunny day a boy and his sister asked their
parents if they might walk to their cousin's house.
The parents said yes. On the way they saw two
dogs and three squirrels and one kitten. The
squirrels ran away, but the dogs and the kitten
were friendly.

Good_____
Fair_____
Poor_____

49

FIRST LEVEL

The children asked their father to build a fire in the fireplace. He used newspapers and dry twigs and logs.

Good_____
Fair_____
Poor_____

SECOND LEVEL

The children asked their father to build a fire in the fireplace. First, he crumpled up newspapers. Then, on top of the newspapers he put dry twigs. Last, he put on three big logs.

Good_____
Fair_____
Poor_____

THIRD LEVEL

One rainy afternoon the children asked their father to build a fire in the fireplace. First, he crumpled up newspapers. Then, on top of the newspapers he put dry twigs. Last, he put on three big logs. The fire was warm and beautiful.

Good_____
Fair_____
Poor_____

50

FIRST LEVEL

A little boy had two ice-cream cones. He gave one to his best friend, and he ate the other one himself.

Good_____
Fair_____
Poor_____

SECOND LEVEL

A little boy had two quarters. He walked to the store and bought two ice-cream cones. He gave one to his best friend, and he ate the other one himself.

Good_____
Fair_____
Poor_____

THIRD LEVEL

A little boy had two quarters. He walked to the store and bought two chocolate ice-cream cones. He gave one to his best friend, and he ate the other one himself. "It is fun to share with good friends," he said.

Good_____
Fair_____
Poor_____

51

FIRST LEVEL

The busy mother asked, "Will you set the table for me?" The helpful little boy said, "Yes, Mother, right away."

Good_____
Fair_____
Poor_____

SECOND LEVEL

The mother was very busy, so she asked her little boy to set the table for dinner. The helpful little boy put knives, forks and spoons on the table. "What else may I do, Mother?" he asked.

Good_____
Fair_____
Poor_____

THIRD LEVEL

The mother was very busy, so she asked her little boy to set the table for dinner. The helpful little boy put knives, forks and spoons on the table. "What else may I do, Mother?" he asked, "That's all, and thank you very much," replied Mother.

Good_____
Fair_____
Poor_____

52

FIRST LEVEL

On Thanksgiving Day the family went downtown to see a parade. The children liked the clowns best of all.

Good_____
Fair_____
Poor_____

SECOND LEVEL

On Thanksgiving Day the family went downtown to see a parade. Mother liked the marching bands. Father liked the beautiful floats. The children liked the clowns best of all.

Good_____
Fair_____
Poor_____

THIRD LEVEL

On Thanksgiving Day the family went downtown to see a parade. Mother liked the marching bands. Father liked the beautiful floats. The children liked the clowns best of all. After the parade the family went home and ate turkey and pumpkin pie.

Good_____
Fair_____
Poor_____

53

FIRST LEVEL

The boy went to the lake with his fishing pole. He caught a big fish. His father cooked it for supper.

Good_____
Fair_____
Poor_____

SECOND LEVEL

The boy went to the lake with his fishing pole. He caught a big fish. His father cleaned it and fried it for supper. Everyone said it was delicious.

Good_____
Fair_____
Poor_____

THIRD LEVEL

The boy went to the lake with his fishing pole. He put a worm on a hook and dropped it into the water. He caught a big fish. His father cleaned it and fried it for supper. Everyone said it was delicious.

Good_____
Fair_____
Poor_____

54

FIRST LEVEL

The little boy wanted to ride to the store on his bicycle. His mother said, "No, not yet. Wait until you are older."

Good_____
Fair_____
Poor_____

SECOND LEVEL

The little boy wanted to ride to the store on his bicycle. His mother said, "No, not yet. Wait until you are 12 years old and have learned all the safety rules."

Good_____
Fair_____
Poor_____

THIRD LEVEL

The little boy wanted to ride to the store on his bicycle. His mother said, "No, not yet. When you are 12 years old and have learned all the safety rules, then you may ride your bike to the store all by yourself."

Good_____
Fair_____
Poor_____

55

FIRST LEVEL

Three children and their mother and father drove
to the airport. A big silver plane landed, and
Grandmother got off.

Good_____
Fair_____
Poor_____

SECOND LEVEL

Three children and their mother and father drove
to the airport. They watched many planes take off
and land. Finally, a big silver plane landed, and
Grandmother got off.

Good_____
Fair_____
Poor_____

THIRD LEVEL

Three children and their mother and father drove
to the airport. They watched many planes take off
and land. Finally, a big silver plane landed, and
Grandmother got off. Everyone was happy to
have Grandmother come for a long visit.

Good_____
Fair_____
Poor_____

56

FIRST LEVEL

The little boy needed a haircut. His mother took him to the barbershop. He sat very still while the barber cut his hair.

Good_____
Fair_____
Poor_____

SECOND LEVEL

The little boy needed a haircut. His mother took him to the barbershop. He sat very still while the barber cut his hair. Then the barber gave him a piece of bubble gum.

Good_____
Fair_____
Poor_____

THIRD LEVEL

The little boy needed a haircut. His mother took him to the barbershop. He saw a tall red-and-white-striped pole in front of the shop. He sat very still while the barber cut his hair. Then the barber gave him a piece of bubble gum.

Good_____
Fair_____
Poor_____

57

FIRST LEVEL

The children were very thirsty. Their mother said they could have lemonade or chocolate milk. They chose chocolate milk.

Good_____
Fair_____
Poor_____

SECOND LEVEL

The children were very thirsty. Their mother said they could have lemonade or chocolate milk or ginger ale. They decided to have chocolate milk. It was cold and tasted good. They all remembered to say thank you.

Good_____
Fair_____
Poor_____

THIRD LEVEL

The children were very thirsty. Their mother said they could have lemonade or chocolate milk or ginger ale. They decided to have chocolate milk. It was cold and tasted good. Each drank two glassfuls and then remembered to say thank you to Mother.

Good_____
Fair_____
Poor_____

58

FIRST LEVEL

The little boy dropped a glass. It broke into many pieces. He was sorry and helped his father sweep up the broken glass.

Good_____
Fair_____
Poor_____

SECOND LEVEL

The little boy dropped a glass. It broke into many pieces. He was sorry and helped his father sweep up the broken glass because he did not want anyone to get hurt.

Good_____
Fair_____
Poor_____

THIRD LEVEL

The little boy was drinking milk. He dropped the glass, which broke into many pieces. He was sorry. He got a broom and a dustpan and helped his father sweep up the broken glass because he did not want anyone to get hurt.

Good_____
Fair_____
Poor_____

59

FIRST LEVEL

The family was going on a picnic. Then it began
to rain. "Let's go to the movies instead," said
Father.

Good_____
Fair_____
Poor_____

SECOND LEVEL

It was Sunday afternoon. The family was going on
a picnic. Dark clouds gathered. Then it began
to rain. "Let's go to the movies instead," said
Father.

Good_____
Fair_____
Poor_____

THIRD LEVEL

It was Sunday afternoon. The family decided to go
on a picnic. Everyone started to pack a lunch.
Dark clouds gathered. Then it began to rain hard.
"Let's go to the movies instead," said Father.
Everyone said yes.

Good_____
Fair_____
Poor_____

60

FIRST LEVEL

Two sisters had a lemonade stand in front of their
house. They sold lemonade for 10 cents a glass.

Good_____
Fair_____
Poor_____

SECOND LEVEL

Two sisters had a lemonade stand in front of their
house. They sold lemonade for 10 cents a glass. At
the end of the afternoon, the lemonade was gone,
and each had 75 cents.

Good_____
Fair_____
Poor_____

THIRD LEVEL

Two sisters had a lemonade stand in front of their
house. They sold lemonade for 10 cents a glass,
and they sold cookies for 5 cents apiece. At the
end of the afternoon, all of the lemonade and
cookies were gone, and each girl had 75 cents.

Good_____
Fair_____
Poor_____

61

FIRST LEVEL

The little girl had a new red kite. She took it outside, and the wind blew it high in the sky.

Good_____
Fair_____
Poor_____

SECOND LEVEL

It was a windy day. The little girl had a new red kite. She put a tail on it and took the kite outside. The wind blew it high in the sky.

Good_____
Fair_____
Poor_____

THIRD LEVEL

It was a windy day. The little girl had a new red kite. She put a tail on it and took the kite outside. She held the string very carefully so that the kite would not get tangled in a tree. The wind blew the kite high in the sky.

Good_____
Fair_____
Poor_____

62

FIRST LEVEL

The boy was playing in his yard. He saw a bird's
nest in a tree. Inside the nest were two tiny blue
eggs.

Good_____
Fair_____
Poor_____

SECOND LEVEL

The boy was playing in his yard. He saw a bird's
nest in a maple tree. He climbed the tree and
peeked into the nest. Inside were two tiny blue
eggs. He did not touch them.

Good_____
Fair_____
Poor_____

THIRD LEVEL

The boy was playing in his yard. He saw a bird's
nest in a maple tree. He climbed the tree and
peeked into the nest. Inside were two tiny blue
eggs. He did not touch them because he knew
that soon baby robins would hatch from the eggs.

Good_____
Fair_____
Poor_____

63

FIRST LEVEL

Two sisters wanted popsicles. There was only one
popsicle in the refrigerator. They shared it.

Good____
Fair____
Poor____

SECOND LEVEL

Two sisters wanted popsicles. There was only one
popsicle in the refrigerator. Their mother took a
knife and cut it into two pieces so they could
share it.

Good____
Fair____
Poor____

THIRD LEVEL

Two sisters wanted popsicles. There was only one
popsicle in the refrigerator. They decided to share
it. Their mother took a knife and cut it into two
pieces. Each sister ate one-half of a cherry popsicle.

Good____
Fair____
Poor____

64

FIRST LEVEL

A freight train is very long and carries many things. It always has a locomotive and a caboose.

Good_____
Fair_____
Poor_____

SECOND LEVEL

A freight train is very long and carries many things. It carries tractors and milk and cows. It always has a locomotive and a caboose.

Good_____
Fair_____
Poor_____

THIRD LEVEL

A freight train is very long and carries many things. It carries big logs on a flatcar. It carries milk in a tank car. It carries cows in a cattle car. A freight train always has a locomotive and a caboose.

Good_____
Fair_____
Poor_____

65

FIRST LEVEL

Today most people travel on planes. Years ago
most people traveled on trains for both short and
long trips.

Good_____
Fair_____
Poor_____

SECOND LEVEL

Today most people travel on planes. Years ago
most people traveled on trains for both short and
long trips. Dining cars on the trains served breakfast, lunch and dinner.

Good_____
Fair_____
Poor_____

THIRD LEVEL

Today most people travel on planes. Years ago
most people traveled on trains for both short and
long trips. Dining cars on the trains served breakfast, lunch and dinner. Trains also had Pullman
cars, in which people could sleep overnight.

Good_____
Fair_____
Poor_____

66

FIRST LEVEL

A boy had a pet turtle. It moved very slowly. It liked to sleep in the warm sunshine and to catch flies for its supper.

Good_____
Fair_____
Poor_____

SECOND LEVEL

A boy had a pet turtle. It moved very slowly. It liked to take naps in the warm sunshine. The turtle caught mosquitoes and flies and ate them for supper.

Good_____
Fair_____
Poor_____

THIRD LEVEL

A boy found a turtle in the lake. He took it home for a pet. It moved very slowly. It liked to take naps in the warm sunshine. The turtle caught mosquitoes and flies and ate them for supper. One day the boy took it back to the lake and let it go.

Good_____
Fair_____
Poor_____

67

FIRST LEVEL

A boy fell out of a tree and broke his arm. The doctor put the arm in a cast. In five weeks it was healed.

Good_____
Fair_____
Poor_____

SECOND LEVEL

A boy fell out of a tree and broke his arm. His mother quickly took him to the doctor. The doctor put the arm in a cast. In five weeks it was healed.

Good_____
Fair_____
Poor_____

THIRD LEVEL

A boy fell out of a tree and broke his left arm. His mother quickly took him to the doctor. The doctor put the arm in a cast. The boy could still eat and do his school work with his right hand. In five weeks the arm was healed, and the doctor took the cast off.

Good_____
Fair_____
Poor_____

68

FIRST LEVEL

The boy and the girl wanted to eat lunch outside. Their father fixed a tray with two sandwiches, two glasses of milk and two bananas.

Good_____
Fair_____
Poor_____

SECOND LEVEL

The boy and the girl wanted to eat lunch outside. Their father fixed a tray. On the tray were two sandwiches, two glasses of chocolate milk and two bananas. The children ate all the food.

Good_____
Fair_____
Poor_____

THIRD LEVEL

The boy and the girl wanted to eat lunch outside. They asked their father to fix a tray. On the tray he put two peanut butter and jelly sandwiches, two glasses of chocolate milk and two bananas. The children sat on the grass and ate all the food.

Good_____
Fair_____
Poor_____

69

FIRST LEVEL

The little girl wanted to learn to use the telephone. Her older sister showed her how to dial a
telephone number.

Good____
Fair____
Poor____

SECOND LEVEL

The little girl wanted to learn to use the telephone. Her older sister showed her how to dial a
telephone number. Soon she was able to call her
best friend and her grandfather.

Good____
Fair____
Poor____

THIRD LEVEL

The little girl wanted to learn to use the telephone. Her older sister showed her how to dial a
telephone number. Soon she was able to call her
best friend, who lived down the street, and her
grandfather, who lived in another town.

Good____
Fair____
Poor____

70

FIRST LEVEL

The eye doctor looked at the boy's eyes very carefully. She decided the boy needed to wear glasses to see better.

Good_____
Fair_____
Poor_____

SECOND LEVEL

The eye doctor looked at the boy's eyes very carefully. She decided the boy needed to wear glasses. When the boy put on his new glasses, he could see much better.

Good_____
Fair_____
Poor_____

THIRD LEVEL

The eye doctor looked at the boy's eyes very carefully. She decided the boy needed to wear glasses. When the boy put on his new glasses, he could see much better. His teacher said, "How grown up you look in your new glasses!"

Good_____
Fair_____
Poor_____

71

FIRST LEVEL

The little boy came into the house from playing outside. He was very muddy. The baby sitter said it was time for a bath.

Good_____
Fair_____
Poor_____

SECOND LEVEL

The little boy came into the house from playing outside. He was very muddy. The baby sitter said it was time for a bath. The boy played in the tub with his boats. Soon he was all clean.

Good_____
Fair_____
Poor_____

THIRD LEVEL

The little boy made many mud pies. When he came into the house, he was very muddy. The baby sitter put some bubble bath into the tub and filled the tub with warm water. The boy played with the bubbles and his boats. Soon he was all clean.

Good_____
Fair_____
Poor_____

72

FIRST LEVEL

The mother decided to teach the boy and the girl how to make a bed. She smoothed the sheets and tucked in the blankets.

Good_____
Fair_____
Poor_____

SECOND LEVEL

The mother decided to teach the boy and the girl how to make a bed. First, she smoothed the sheets and tucked in the blankets. Then, she placed two pillows at the head of the bed.

Good_____
Fair_____
Poor_____

THIRD LEVEL

The mother decided to teach the boy and the girl how to make a bed. First, she smoothed the sheets and tucked in the blankets. Then, she placed two pillows at the head of the bed. After she left the room, the boy and the girl bounced on the bed.

Good_____
Fair_____
Poor_____

73

FIRST LEVEL

The family went to the zoo. They saw elephants and monkeys. They took a ride on the zoo train.

Good_____
Fair_____
Poor_____

SECOND LEVEL

The family went to the zoo. They saw elephants and monkeys and many other animals. Then they took a ride on the zoo train, which had a loud whistle.

Good_____
Fair_____
Poor_____

THIRD LEVEL

The family went to the zoo. They saw elephants and monkeys and giraffes and many other animals. They ate popcorn. Then they took a ride on the zoo train, which had a loud whistle.

Good_____
Fair_____
Poor_____

74

FIRST LEVEL

The mother and the father were going out. A sitter came to stay with the children. She read them stories.

Good_____
Fair_____
Poor_____

SECOND LEVEL

The mother and the father were going out. A sitter came to stay with the children. She read them stories. The children hoped she would come again soon.

Good_____
Fair_____
Poor_____

THIRD LEVEL

The mother and the father were going out. A sitter came to stay with the children. She read stories and played games and made popcorn. She was so very nice that the children hoped their mother and father would let the sitter come again soon.

Good_____
Fair_____
Poor_____

75

FIRST LEVEL

A little girl got roller skates for her birthday. She practiced very hard, and soon she could skate up and down the sidewalk.

Good_____
Fair_____
Poor_____

SECOND LEVEL

A little girl got roller skates for her birthday. At first she could not stand up in them. She practiced very hard, and soon she could skate up and down the sidewalk.

Good_____
Fair_____
Poor_____

THIRD LEVEL

A little girl got roller skates for her birthday. She put them on right away. At first she had difficulty standing up in them and fell down often. She practiced very hard, and soon she could skate up and down the sidewalk. Then she learned to skate backwards.

Good_____
Fair_____
Poor_____

SECTION TWO:

Helping the Child Learn How to Listen

Exercises

HELPING THE CHILD LEARN HOW TO LISTEN

Listening can be taught as a skill, just as reading, writing and spelling are taught. The following are exercises designed to help the child learn to listen, to follow directions and to develop auditory memory.

In all of these exercises it will be necessary for the instructor (teacher or parent) to give directions. Several important points should be observed. Instructions should be kept simple, using as few words as possible. Many times demonstrating a task is more effective than describing it, although it should always be borne in mind that helping the child to learn to follow directions is one of the goals of the exercises.

All instructions should be aimed at the child's level of comprehension. Sometimes it may be necessary to reword them to the child's frame of reference.

Since these exercises are designed for the child with auditory perceptual problems, it is important to wait for slow processing or delayed responses.

The training sessions must be kept short—no more than 15 or 20 minutes. The instructor must watch the youngster for signs of boredom. If bored, a child will not work at listening. A training session should be brought to a close while interest is still high so that the child will look forward to another period of similar activity.

The author wishes to acknowledge the contributions of the Achievement Center for Children, Purdue University, and of the Department of Special Education, Southern Connecticut State College, where the concepts for many of these exercises were designed and developed.

1

A logical starting point in developing the skill of listening is a game of "being quiet." Not only the voice but the entire body stays still so that no sound is made. The child remains in this total silence for a few seconds, gradually increasing the length of time to two minutes.

The instructor then steps out of the room and whispers the child's name or a simple command. The child comes if his or her name is whispered or performs suitably if a command is whispered.

In a group situation, the teacher instructs the class to be quiet and to listen for a specific sound, such as a ticking clock or metronome. Other sounds from the building or the playground can then be identified and categorized. For example, sounds of children playing games can be "loud and happy" sounds; those of a custodian sweeping the floor can be "soft, swishing and busy" sounds.

2

Inside. The child sits quietly, listens and decides the direction from which a sound is coming. He or she is then instructed to look for whatever is making the sound. Examples: running water, an alarm clock, a transistor radio.

Outside. The child is directed to sit quietly, with eyes closed, and to listen for a prescribed length of time. He or she then identifies and lists the sounds heard. Examples: an airplane, a car, birds. This game can be played competitively in a group. The child who hears a sound no other child has heard gets an extra point, etc.

Discussions should be held on the *degree* or *intensity* of sound; for instance, a truck sounds loud as it drives by a school, but the sound diminishes as it gets farther and farther away.

Imitation of familiar sounds should be encouraged in a wide range of volume from very loud to very soft.

3

Two different sound-making objects are introduced. The child is allowed to inspect and manipulate each. Examples: a bell, a metal cricket, a tambourine.

The items are then concealed under a table or placed elsewhere out of the youngster's line of vision. (Or the child is requested to keep his or her eyes closed.) One of the items is sounded, and the child attempts to identify the object.

A new, third item is introduced. Again, one item is sounded, and the child tries to determine which one of the three has made the noise.

A subtle variation employs bells of different sizes and tones. The child identifies "big bell," "middle-sized bell" or "little bell" according to the individual sound. This provides an opportunity to deal in the additional concepts of large, small, loud, soft, etc.

In a group situation, the members of the class are instructed to close their eyes. The teacher moves from place to place throughout the room and calls the name of a child, who must point in the direction from which the sound emanates.

4

The instructor gives a command and performs with the child: "Stand." "Sit." "Kneel." The command might relate to the identification of body parts: "Point to your shoulders." "Point to your knees."

Or, the instructor gives a command but does *not* perform with the child.

In a group situation, the instructor tells a story and the children raise their hands whenever a part of the body is mentioned.

Sample story: The little boy looks at the *hands* of a clock. He *knows* (nose) it is time for lunch. "*I* (eye) am so hungry *I* (eye) could eat as much as an *army*," he says. He goes to the table, but one *leg* of his chair is broken. He walks *back* to the kitchen to get another chair. Then he goes a*head* and eats his lunch.

5

The instructor calls out a series of related items. Examples: numbers, fruits, vegetables, boys' and girls' names, colors. The child repeats the series. The task should be continually upgraded. Once the child can handle a series of four, the list should be increased to five, etc.

An interesting variation of this exercise is to ask the child to *reverse* the series. Example: (Instructor) "Nine, three, one, eight." (Child) "Eight, one, three, nine."

The instructor calls out a series of objects, and the child picks out the word which does not belong. Examples: apple, grape, peach, corn, banana; elephant, tiger, robin, giraffe, lion; airplane, car, house, truck, train.

6

The child is shown pictures of various farm and domestic animals. The instructor makes a sound representative of one of the animals, and the child points to the appropriate picture.

A discussion is conducted concerning which animals make loud sounds (a lion roars) and which ones make soft sounds (a snake hisses). Low sounds (moo) and high sounds (meow) are compared.

The instructor slowly chants a list of animals. The child claps whenever he or she hears the name of an animal that lives on a farm (or in the jungle or in a zoo).

7

The instructor gives a simple command. Example: "Walk slowly to the table." The child repeats the command, then carries through with the action required. (If the instructor desires, the child's repeating of the command may be omitted.)

If the child has reached the appropriate level, two simple commands may be given in the preceding activity. Example: "Walk slowly to the table and pick up the book."

Likewise, if the instructor deems it suitable, three simple commands may be used. Example: "Walk slowly to the table, pick up the book and bring it to me."

Tasks and combinations of tasks should be varied. Commands should be given with the pitch and volume of the voice lowered.

Another activity involves assembling a group of familiar grocery items on a table. One child is chosen to be the "clerk." Another child "telephones" the "store" and places an order (the number of items ordered depends on the ability of the children). The "clerk" then delivers the order to the "customer."

8

With eyes closed, the child tries to identify the voices of members of the family or playmates or classmates. If the child is fairly skilled at the game, the participants may try to disguise their voices.

With the child's eyes shut, the instructor repeats one sentence, varying it in inflection and intonation. The child decides if the voice sounds happy, surprised, tired, sorry, etc.

In a group situation, the instructor tells the story of "The Three Bears" or "The Three Billy Goats Gruff," using variations in pitch to imitate the voices of the three central animal characters. Then, one child is selected to imitate the voice of one of the animals, and the class guesses which bear or goat the child is pretending to be.

9

Sounds of nature should be pointed out to the child as they occur, and time should be taken for the youngster to sit quietly and listen to these sounds. Examples: wind, as it blows through the trees or bangs a shutter; rain, as it varies from light to heavy; water, as it rushes or falls; dry leaves, as they are crumpled underfoot; fire, as it crackles.

By using certain materials, the child can imitate some sounds of nature. Examples: crumpling cellophane to sound like fire burning; blowing through a tube to sound like wind blowing; slowly dropping a handful of dried beans into a container of water to sound like raindrops splashing into a puddle.

Children's poems that incorporate the sounds of nature can be read aloud, followed by discussions of words that sound like what they denote. Examples: slush, breeze, thunder.

10

An object is hidden in the room. Instead of using the standard clues of "hot" when the child is near the object and "cold" when he or she is far away, the instructor makes a sound to which the child listens carefully. When the youngster is near the object, the sound becomes louder. As he or she moves farther away, the sound grows softer. Examples of sounds: "buzz-z-z-z"; "click, click, click."

The sound can be related to the object which is hidden. For instance, a toy locomotive is hidden, and the sound is "chug, chug" or "choo, choo"; a picture of an animal is hidden, and the appropriate sound made.

A game of Echo provides an effective activity. One child chants a word or a sentence; another child across the room echoes it in softer tones. Instead of words or sentences, taps or claps in a rhythmic sequence can be employed.

11

Any games are appropriate which use auditory clues combined with movement. Examples: Simon Says; Here We Go 'Round the Mulberry Bush; Loob-de-Loo; Monkey See, Monkey Do.

Voice volume can be varied during these games. A game can be sung or chanted in a whisper, in a soft voice, in a normal voice or in a loud voice. Occasionally the child should be allowed to choose the "voice" to be used.

A variation of Simon Says substitutes sound-producing actions for the touching of body parts. Example: "Simon says: 'Clap your hands; stamp your feet; click your tongue; snap your fingers; sneeze; whistle; hum.'"

12

Reading aloud to the child should be a daily habit. The technique in reading for pure sound enjoyment differs from that used when the child is to re-tell the material as described earlier. The instructor should read slowly, distinctly and with good inflection. As much expression and flavor as possible should be injected into the reading.

Recommended reading material: stories with opportunities for the reader to create sound effects; poems with strong rhythm and rhyme schemes.

Also, records may be played that include sounds of animals, machines, traffic or nature.

The child may be asked to listen with eyes closed and to visualize what is making each sound.

13

The instructor says, "I am going to say some words. Listen and tell me which word is in the middle." A group of three words is then spoken. The task can be somewhat simplified if the first and last words not only rhyme but also have the same number of syllables. Example: map, pencil, tap.

The task can be varied by asking the child to name the first and/or last word in a spoken sentence. In this case the sentence can be quite long.

To increase difficulty even more, two sentences can be spoken, with a significant pause between them, after which the child is asked to name the first and/or last word in each of the sentences.

14

The child is given an activity sheet with 10 or 12 simple illustrations, widely spaced. The instructor calls out a word. The child circles the matching picture. This can be done with nouns or verbs.

For the older child, the activity sheet can contain printed words rather than illustrations. Numerals can also be used.

15

Out of the child's line of vision, the instructor drops coins or beads, one at a time, into a container. The child listens quietly and carefully and then answers with the number of objects dropped.

Alternate activity: Out of the child's line of vision, the instructor drops objects into a container. The child listens and then drops the same number of objects into another container. In a group situation, the class monitors this activity and announces whether or not the child has dropped the correct number of items.

Note: It is best to start with just three or four items until the ability level of the class or individual members has been established.

16

The child is given three objects that are identical except for color. Example: a red block, a blue block, a green block. The instructor calls out the three colors slowly. The child arranges the items in the required sequence. The task can be made more difficult by increasing the number of objects or by calling out the colors more rapidly.